Virginia Woolf's

Mrs. Dalloway

Text by
David M. Gracer
(M.A., University of Wyoming)
Department of English
Mercy College
Dobbs Ferry, New York

Illustrations by
Karen Pica

Research & Education Association

MAXnotes® for
MRS. DALLOWAY

Printed in the United States of America

Library of Congress Catalog Card Number 96-67425

International Standard Book Number 0-87891-032-8

MAXnotes® is a registered trademark of
Research & Education Association, Piscataway, New Jersey 08854

What **MAXnotes**® *Will Do for You*

This book is intended to help you absorb the essential contents and features of Virginia Woolf's *Mrs. Dalloway* and to help you gain a thorough understanding of the work. The book has been designed to do this more quickly and effectively than any other study guide.

For best results, this **MAXnotes** book should be used as a companion to the actual work, not instead of it. The interaction between the two will greatly benefit you.

To help you in your studies, this book presents the most up-to-date interpretations of every section of the actual work, followed by questions and fully explained answers that will enable you to analyze the material critically. The questions also will help you to test your understanding of the work and will prepare you for discussions and exams.

Meaningful illustrations are included to further enhance your understanding and enjoyment of the literary work. The illustrations are designed to place you into the mood and spirit of the work's settings.

The **MAXnotes** also include summaries, character lists, explanations of plot, and section-by-section analyses. A biography of the author and discussion of the work's historical context will help you put this literary piece into the proper perspective of what is taking place.

The use of this study guide will save you the hours of preparation time that would ordinarily be required to arrive at a complete grasp of this work of literature. You will be well prepared for classroom discussions, homework, and exams. The guidelines that are included for writing papers and reports on various topics will prepare you for any added work which may be assigned.

The **MAXnotes** will take your grades "to the max."

Dr. Max Fogiel
Program Director

Contents

> **Each Part includes List of Characters,
> Summary, Analysis, Study Questions and
> Answers, and Suggested Essay Topics.**

SECTION ONE

Introduction

The Life and Work of Virginia Woolf

Virginia Woolf was born Adeline Virginia Stephen in London on January 25, 1882, and died by suicide on March 12, 1941. She came from a family of writers: her father, Sir Leslie Stephen, was a prominent writer during Queen Victoria's reign, and her maternal grandfather was William Thackeray, author of *Vanity Fair*.

Virginia Stephen and her sister Vanessa were interested in the arts from their childhoods, Vanessa in painting and Virginia in writing. Their mother's death in 1895 took a great toll on them, and they were sexually abused by their stepbrother, George Duckworth. Virginia suffered her first mental breakdown when she was thirteen years old and several were to follow throughout her life.

The Stephen sisters settled in Bloomsbury, a section of London that was an unofficial artist's colony before and after World War I. Virginia married Leonard Woolf in 1912, and in 1917 they started Hogarth Press which operated out of their home in London. Virginia Woolf worked as a typesetter and reader for the press from 1917 to 1937. In addition to the works of the Woolfs' friends, such as E.M. Forster and Katherine Mansfield, many of Virginia Woolf's books, including *Mrs. Dalloway*, were first issued by the Hogarth Press.

Woolf was prolific, with over 35 essay collections, biographies, and novels being published during her lifetime. Her journals and her many other books were published posthumously. Although she is best known for her novels, Woolf's essays are often anthologized. The essays reveal Woolf's interest in social questions as they relate to the arts and women writers. She attacked what she considered outdated ideas about literature, arguing that literary expression should not overlook any aspect of human life. While she claimed that the right to vote made no difference to her, Woolf wrote that women must never be silenced. Throughout her texts, Woolf promotes the role as author for literary women.

Despite a successful career, Woolf's private life was deeply and consistently troubled. Her comfortable marriage did not assuage periods of depression, prompted by self-doubts and, to a lesser extent, world affairs. Recalling the horrors of World War I, Woolf and others watched developments in Germany, and dreaded the prospects of another brutal war and the triumph of anti-semitism.

Also, having endured several breakdowns, Woolf knew the toll mental instability exacted from herself and on her husband. Fearing of another breakdown, Virginia Woolf filled her pockets with stones one day in March 1941, to make herself heavier when she leapt into the River Ouse.

Historical Background

The world of *Mrs. Dalloway* is dualistic, meaning that it concerns two opposites. Though London is calm, basking in sunlight and peace following World War I, the reader sees the inner struggles of the characters, who are fraught with contradiction and unhappiness.

The war is a real, tangible presence in the novel. Memories of it are still fresh, in the comments about the sons and husbands killed and in an example of war's legacy: Septimus Warren Smith, a soldier who had been traumatized by the violence he had witnessed. In Woolf's time, victims of post-battle stress were called "shellshocked," and their mental conditions were misunderstood.

The novel reflects the work of Sigmund Freud, a German doctor who revolutionized the new field of psychology with the publication of his first work, *An Introduction to Psychoanalysis*, in 1916. The Woolfs were familiar with Freud's work, having published translations of his writings.

Mrs. Dalloway occupies an important place in modern literature. It follows a principle of Henry James, an American writer who spent most of his life in Europe. He described the power of situating the action of a novel in the mental life of the characters. That *Mrs. Dalloway* takes place in a single day prompts comparisons to James Joyce's *Ulysses*, an epic examination of a day as lived by three citizens of Dublin, Ireland. While Woolf said she disliked the novel, it must have influenced her direction in plot, characterization, and the transmission of sensibility.

Master List of Characters

Clarissa Dalloway—*A woman giving a party on the evening of the day with which the novel is concerned; She is busily arranging details for her big evening. She is 52-years-old.*

Richard Dalloway—*Clarissa's husband, a well respected and powerful public official; He is 55-years-old.*

Peter Walsh—*An old friend of Clarissa's who just returned from a trip to India; There was some chance of romantic involvment between Peter and Clarissa, long before. He is 53-years-old.*

Hugh Whitbread—*An old friend of Clarissa's; Condescending and arrogant, he is disliked by most of the characters who know him. He is 51-years-old.*

Sally Seton—*An old friend of Clarissa's; While the two have been out of touch for a long time, Sally was once very important to Clarissa. She arrives at the party as Lady Rosseter.*

Septimus Warren Smith—*A man who returned from World War I before the action of the novel; He is effected by his experiences there. He is approximately 30-years-old.*

Lucrezia Warren Smith (Rezia)—*Septimus' wife; small and nervous, especially about her husband; She still possesses some beauty. He brought her to England from Italy, and she makes hats. She is 24-years-old.*

Dr. Holmes—*Septimus' doctor, recommended by Mrs. Filmer, the Smith's cook; Unable to help his patient, the doctor calls in Sir William Bradshaw.*

Sir William Bradshaw—*The specialist called in to cure Septimus; He has plans to send Septimus to a special home, where he will have a chance to get a good rest.*

Evans—*A man who died in the great war; He was a close friend of Septimus Warren Smith.*

Lady Bruton—*A vivacious woman who invites Richard Dalloway and Hugh Whitbread to her home for luncheon. She frequently writes letters to the London Times, and relies on the talents of these two men to assist her.*

Elizabeth Dalloway—*The daughter of Clarissa and Richard Dalloway. She is 17-years-old, and strangely beautiful.*

Doris Kilman—*A friend of Elizabeth's; An older woman, she is frail, grasping, and religious, much to the chagrin of Elizabeth's parents. She seems to have strong feelings about Elizabeth.*

Mrs. Filmer—*The Smiths' cook; She recommends Dr. Holmes. She has a married, pregnant daughter named Mrs. Peters, for whom Lucrezia makes a hat.*

Maisie Johnson—*A young woman who has come to London from Scotland; She is lost and perplexed when she sees Septimus and Lucrezia.*

Mrs. Dempster—*An older woman who observes Maisie Johnson and the Smiths; Having lived a demanding life, she is full of advice, which she keeps to herself.*

Milly Brush—*Lady Bruton's secretary; She likes Richard Dalloway but condemns Hugh Whitbread. She has a brother in South Africa.*

Lucy—*Clarissa's maid.*

Agnes—*The Smiths' servant girl.*

Sylvia—*Clarissa's late sister.*

Summary of the Novel

Virginia Woolf's *Mrs. Dalloway* is the story of a day in June 1923, as lived by a few London citizens. There is a calm in the air; people are enjoying a sense of peace and remembering their lives from before the long and bitter World War I.

Mrs. Dalloway is a novel about people's inner lives. It does not possess a vivid plot; the actual events are secondary to what people spend much of their time pondering: memories, regrets, and hopes. Almost all of the main characters wonder about what might have been. The novel is told from the viewpoint of an omniscient and invisible narrator.

Most of the characters are well off financially, and have considerable leisure time. Yet they are quite busy with the business of being alive, which includes asking questions of their internal and external worlds. These questions do not always make them happy. On the contrary, most of the characters are unhappy for all or part of their day.

In keeping with Woolf's interest in psychology, sexuality is a theme in the novel. Several of the characters are divided in their feelings towards love, and this contributes to their ambivalence.

The actions of the novel are simple: Clarissa Dalloway is hosting a formal party. She sees Peter Walsh, who has returned from India, and drops in for a visit. This meeting, and many other moments in the day, make Clarissa think about the past and the choices she has made. Clarissa's husband, Richard, has meetings and lunches, and their daughter Elizabeth has similar plans herself. Another Londoner, Septimus Warren Smith, is having a bad day, and so is his wife Lucrezia. Septimus is obsessed with his memories of Evans, a friend who was killed in the war. He is also convinced that unseen forces are sending him messages. Lucrezia is taking Septimus to two doctors, neither of whom can do much to cure him. Septimus kills himself later in the day, to escape his doctors, and because he feels he has no other alternative.

Clarissa's party is a success. The Prime Minister arrives, and this is considered a great honor. In the midst of her success as a hostess, she hears of Septimus' suicide. Although she never met him, the news moves her to the core of her being.

Estimated Reading Time

The average silent reading rate is 250 to 300 words per minute, making the total reading time for this novel about five hours. Yet the student must remember that Mrs. *Dalloway* is a relatively abstract novel. It uses unusual narrative techniques and lacks the action and drama you may be accustomed to. A novel as subtle and complex as this requires more than merely enough time. A combination of endurance and sensitivity is needed to ensure success.

There are no chapter breaks in *Mrs. Dalloway*, and Woolf's method of centering on the minds of her characters can make *Mrs. Dalloway* a challenging novel. Since there are no chapter breaks in the original work, the MAXnotes guide is divided into eighteen parts. The book is divided as follows:

Part One:

From the beginning of the novel until the sentence:

"Dear, those motor cars," said Miss Pym, going to the window to look, and coming back and smiling apologetically with her hands full of sweet peas, as if those motor cars, those tyres of motorcars, were all her fault."

Part Two:

From the sentence:

"The violent explosion which made Mrs. Dalloway jump and Miss Pym go to the window and apologize came from a motor car which had drawn to the side of the pavement precisely opposite Mulberry's show window."
To the sentence:

"And now, curving up and up, straight up, like something mounting in ecstasy, in pure delight, out from behind poured white smoke looping, writing a T, an O, an F."

Part Three:

From the sentence:

"What are they looking at?" said Clarissa Dalloway to the maid who opened her door."
To the sentence:

"She had worn them at Hatfield; at Buckingham Palace."

Part Four:

From the sentence:

"Quiet descended on her, calm, content, as her needle, drawing silk smoothly to its gentle pause, connected the green folds

together and attached them, very lightly, to the belt."
To the phrase:
    "as Peter Walsh shut the door."

Part Five:
From the sentence:
    "Remember my party, remember my party, said Peter Walsh as he stepped down the street, speaking to himself rhythmically, in time with the flow of the sound, the direct downright sound of Big Ben striking the half hour."
To the sentence:
    "But to whom does the solitary traveler make reply?"

Part Six:
From the sentence:
    "So the elderly nurse knitted over the sleeping baby in Regent's Park."
To the sentence:
    "He never saw her again."

Part Seven:
From the sentence:
    "It was awful, he cried, awful, awful!"
To the sentence:
    "As he sat smiling at the dead man in the grey suit, the quarter struck the quarter to twelve."

Part Eight:
From the sentence:
    "And that is being young, Peter Walsh thought as he passed them."
To the sentence:
    "There she would sit on the sofa by his side, let him take her hand, give her one kiss. Here he was at the crossing."

Part Nine:
From the phrase:
    "A sound interrupted him; a frail quivering sound,"
To the sentence:
    "He gave in."

Part Ten:
From the sentence:
    "Nothing could rouse him."
To the sentence:
    "But Rezia Warren Smith cried, walking down Harley Street, that she did not like that man."

Part Eleven:
From the phrases:
    "Shredding and slicing, dividing and subdividing, the clocks of Harley Street nibbled at the June day,"
To the phrase:
    "he would go straight to her, in Westminster."

Part Twelve:
From the sentence:
    "But he wanted to come in holding something."
To the sentence:
    "After that, how unbelievable death was! that it must end; and no one in the whole world would know how she loved it all; how, every instant..."

Part Thirteen:
From the sentence:
    "The door opened."
To the phrases:
    "with a final twist, bowing her head very politely, she went."

Part Fourteen:

From the sentence:
"She had gone."
To the sentence:
"Calmly and competently, Elizabeth Dalloway mounted the Westminster omnibus."

Part Fifteen:

From the words:
"Going and coming, beckoning, signalling,"
To the sentence:
"So that was Dr. Holmes."

Part Sixteen:

From the sentence:
"One of the triumphs of civilisation, Peter Walsh thought."
To the sentence:
"He opened the big blade of his pocketknife."

Part Seventeen:

From the phrase:
"Lucy came running full tilt downstairs,"
To the phrase:
"she must go up to Lady Bradshaw and say…"

Part Eighteen:

From the sentence:
"But Lady Bradshaw anticipated her."
To the end of the novel.

Teachers will no doubt be sensitive to Woolf's difficult technique, and divide their assignments accordingly. Allow plenty of time to enjoy this great work.

Mrs. Dalloway

Part One

New Characters:

Clarissa Dalloway: *the main character of the novel; spends the day preparing for a party she is hosting that evening*

Hugh Whitbread: *a friend of Clarissa's and of her husband Richard; holds a post in the Royal House; arrogantly self-assured, he is held in contempt by most of the characters in the novel*

Summary

Clarissa Dalloway goes to buy flowers, since Lucy, the maid, is already quite busy. It's a June morning, and Clarissa compares it to the mornings at Bourton, the summer home where she had lived long before. It was there that she knew her closest friends, especially Peter Walsh, whom Clarissa recalls is due back from India some day soon, though she is not sure when.

The day is lovely weather for walking. A man named Scrope Purvis sees Clarissa, and thinks of her as charmingly bird-like. Big Ben, the famous London clock tower, tolls the hour of ten a.m. Clarissa's thoughts flow from one subject to the next, and she sees Hugh Whitbread coming towards her.

Clarissa enjoys seeing Hugh, yet finds him slightly patronizing. Always concerned about looking her best, she feels that his

perfect deportment contrasts with the minute flaws she perceives in herself. They chat about Clarissa's party, and Hugh's wife, Evelyn's health, which as usual is poor. Clarissa commiserates.

After Clarissa and Hugh part, she thinks back to Peter and the others from those years at Bourton. She remembers how Peter detested Hugh, and the fact that Hugh was not completely stupid after all, as Peter had claimed. Clarissa recalls a quotation from Shakespeare, and imagines what she would look like if she had a choice; tall and imposing Clarissa decides, instead of stick-like and insignificant, as Clarissa sees herself.

A glove shop reminds Clarissa of her daughter, Elizabeth, who immediately reminds Clarissa of Doris Kilman, an older and very religious woman who seems to have attached herself to Elizabeth. Thinking about Kilman raises strong feelings of anger in Clarissa, which shock and displease her. Troubled by these emotions, Clarissa enters Mulberry's, the florist, and is immediately soothed by the flowers. She notes the positive effects they seem to have on Miss Pym. While selecting flowers, Clarissa is startled by a car's backfire.

Analysis

The novel begins with its own title, and the reader is plunged into Clarissa's day in the very first sentence. Clarissa is considerate of others and a very active person; this serves to keep her distracted from asking too many questions. Yet despite her errands, she is at the mercy of her memories. She spends much of this day mulling over the past, and the choices that led her to the present in which she lives. One great question in her life is about Peter Walsh, the man whose proposal she refused. The background material comes from both Clarissa's thoughts, and from the invisible narrator, who informs the reader of the characters' pasts.

As well as pondering her personal history, Clarissa thinks about her party. The chapter shows how Clarissa tends to overanalyze her perceptions of herself and of others. People recognize Clarissa and think well of her, but these thoughts do not change the recriminations that occupy part of her daily thoughts. Clarissa understands herself, but she does not seem to like who she is, and her feelings about her past have become obstacles in her present. Contrasted against the dark, brooding conflicts inside Clarissa is the city of London, lovely and filled with the sunshine of the June day.

Study Questions

1. When she hears the sound of windows opening, how old does Clarissa remember being at Bourton?
2. How does Clarissa remember Peter's letters?
3. In what part of London has Clarissa lived for twenty years?
4. What street does Clarissa cross as Big Ben strikes the hour?
5. What is Hugh Whitbread carrying when Clarissa sees him?
6. What is Clarissa oddly conscious of while talking with Hugh?
7. To what does Clarissa liken her hatred of Doris Kilman?
8. Why does Clarissa hate Doris Kilman?
9. What color are the hands of Mrs. Pym, the florist?
10. What does Clarissa assume about the car's backfire?

Answers

1. When she hears the sound of windows opening, Clarissa remembers being eighteen at Bourton.
2. Clarissa remembers Peter's letters as being awfully dull.
3. The part of London in which Clarissa (and her husband and daughter) has lived for twenty years is Westminster.
4. Clarissa crosses Victoria Street as Big Ben strikes the hour.
5. Hugh Whitbread is carrying a despatch box stamped with the Royal Arms when he sees Clarissa.
6. Clarissa is oddly conscious of her hat while talking with Hugh.
7. Clarissa likens her hatred of Doris Kilman to a monster in the woods of her own soul.
8. Clarissa hates Doris Kilman, because the latter is intolerably overbearing. Clarissa feels that "she was never in the room

for five minutes without making you feel her superiority, your inferiority; how poor she was; how rich you were".

9. Mrs. Pym's hands are bright red, as if they had been soaking in cold water with her flowers.

10. Clarissa assumes that the car's backfire was a pistol shot.

Suggested Essay Topics

1. Summarize what Clarissa does and thinks about. What thoughts and actions in this reading section cause her to feel the happiest? To which thoughts does she have the strongest reactions?

2. Summarize London as it is described in this reading. What information and inferences can be drawn about the city?

Part Two

New Characters:

Septimus Warren Smith: *a man who fought in the recent World War, and has not been the same since; acts in a disturbed, disoriented fashion*

Lucrezia Warren Smith: *Septimus' wife, whom he met in Italy; she makes hats, and worries about Septimus and their marriage*

Maisie Johnson: *a young woman recently arrived in London from Edinburgh, Scotland; asks the Smiths for directions, and is bewildered by her glimpse into their unhappiness*

Mrs. Dempster (Carrie): *an older woman who observes Maisie Johnson; she thinks about her life, and believes herself lucky*

Summary

The loud backfire that startles Clarissa comes from the car of an important personage. The people on Bond Street speculate about whose car they see, wondering whether it belongs to an important politician or even a member of the Royal Family. In a philosophical tone, the narrative describes the emotions that the car evokes from those who see it. People perceive that greatness is among them, and that knowledge has a physical effect on them all.

An airplane is heard. Just as with the car backfire, fear is the automatic reaction, even if only momentary, for they think of the war. People then observe puffs of smoke that seem to form words. It seems to be an attempt to sell something, but no one can quite make out the letters.

Septimus and Lucrezia Warren Smith are introduced. Septimus is morose and not listening to his wife, who tries to divert him by pointing out details from their surroundings. Instead of paying attention to the scenery around him, Septimus focuses on mysterious voices, believing that he is receiving secret messages.

Septimus' condition causes great stress in his marriage with Lucrezia, and this tension is observed by Maisie Johnson. A young woman just arrived in London from Edinburgh, Maisie is lost and asks the Smiths for directions. Although she spends just a moment in their vicinity, their unhappiness makes a great impression on her.

Just as Maisie Johnson sees the Smiths, Mrs. Dempster observes Maisie's confusion. She sums up Maisie with the phrase "that girl don't know nothing." Carrie Dempster appraises her life and decides that though she has had a hard life, she would not change lives with any woman she knew. Even so, she longs for a measure of sympathy and even pity, such as a kiss upon her face.

Analysis

The examinations of the car and the airplane are examples of the narrative voice, which is not identified or personified in the novel. Many people's thoughts are stirred by the plane. Its freedom contrasts with the confinement felt by many of the characters.

As far as the feelings of nationalism and pride that the car evokes in the streets of London, we should remember that the people of England felt differently about their "rulers" than they do today. The English having recently emerged from war also contributes to the satisfaction they feel when seeing symbols of their ways of life, such as the car. By contrast, the plane is a symbol of all humankind, transcending mere nationality.

The end of this reading section includes a 127 word sentence, which is far longer than most written sentences. The sentence concerns the mental meanderings of a man standing in front of a cathedral. He wonders about the society of the place and of the people called to perform their duties. The wandering quality of this sentence reflects the workings of the human mind. Woolf disregards standard grammar so as to better transmit how the human mind's use language for its own purposes.

This technique occurs repeatedly in the novel. While it may not seem to be reader friendly, a little effort (reading aloud is helpful, for the sentences contain punctuation to guide the reader through the rhythms of the characters' minds), will allow the reader to grasp the characters' stream of consciousness and how they arrive at their conclusions.

Study Questions

1. Whose car does Edgar J. Watkiss believe has just passed?

2. Who does Lucrezia wonder was in the car?

3. Where does the car proceed?

4. What does Septimus say that so upsets Lucrezia?

5. How does Septimus interpret the smoke letters made by the plane?

6. What does Lucrezia tell her mother, to explain Septimus' behavior?

7. To where does Maisie Johnson ask Septimus and Lucrezia for directions?

8. What question does Maisie Johnson ask herself?

9. What had Mrs. Dempster always longed for?

10. What does the airplane seem to be a symbol of, as Mr. Bentley sees it?

Answers

1. Edgar J. Watkiss believes that the Prime Minister's car has just passed.

2. Lucrezia wonders if the Queen was in the car, perhaps to go shopping.

3. The car proceeds toward Piccadilly, a famous square in London.

4. What Septimus says to upset Lucrezia is, "I will kill myself."

5. Septimus interprets the smoke letters made by the plane to be signals sent to him.

6. To explain Septimus' behavior, Lucrezia tells her mother that "Septimus has been working too hard."

7. Maisie Johnson asks Septimus and Lucrezia for directions to Regent's Park Station.

8. Maisie Johnson asks herself why she hadn't stayed at home, meaning Edinburgh, Scotland.

9. Mrs. Dempster had always longed to see foreign lands.

10. As Mr. Bentley sees it, the airplane is a symbol of man's soul.

Suggested Essay Topics

1. Compare what is known about Clarissa Dalloway with the information and material concerning Septimus Warren Smith. How do their words and actions compare?

2. Consider the scene with Maisie Johnson and Mrs. Dempster. What are your reactions to these characters? What words and actions, or information given about them, created these reactions? What does the scene tell you about people, and about the novel?

Part Three

New Characters:

Sally Seton: *an old friend of Clarissa*

Lucy: *the Dalloway's maid*

Lady Bruton: *vivacious woman who invites Richard Dalloway and Hugh Whitbread to her home for a luncheon*

Richard Dalloway: *Clarissa's husband*

Summary

Returning from the florist, Clarissa finds that Richard is lunching at Lady Bruton's. Excluded and hurt, Clarissa appreciates Lucy's sympathy. The two share a moment of silent communication. Clarissa's disappointment affects her thoughts. She overreacts internally, imagining herself ancient and alone, because she was not invited. She worries about the extent of her social graces.

Climbing the stairs, Clarissa thinks of the attic, where she reads late at night. The couple has an understanding that since Clarissa's unexplained "illness," she sleeps alone, and she feels she has failed Richard because some part of her has kept her apart from him physically. This part of her centers on "a virginity preserved through childhood which clung to her like a sheet." Clarissa's thoughts about love lead directly to Bourton and Sally Seton. Clarissa recalls those times in great detail, both the events and people's comments about what others did. More than anyone else, it is Sally who occupies Clarissa's memories.

Clarissa remembers Peter Walsh, and wonders what he might say about her now. She thinks about her age, and she ponders her own face. She finally shrugs off these broodings, and selects the dress she wishes to wear for that night's party, but it's torn. Planning to repair it later, she descends the stairs and talks to Lucy about the silver.

Analysis

This reading section contains the first highly detailed account of Bourton, where Clarissa once lived. Woolf makes the past at least as important to the characters as the present. It is an important factor in their lives, and often a major obstacle to their happiness.

Many memories about Bourton regard a particular summer, full of incidents and conversations that occurred thirty-four years before. We learn that Clarissa is 52-years-old in the novel's present, and remembered being eighteen at the beginning of the novel,

when the sounds of windows opening "transported her back" to Bourton.

These memories raise questions about love and the mystery of emotions. From her habit of reading alone late at night, the reader can suppose that Clarissa's marriage with Richard is not especially sexual. That Clarissa reads about Baron Marbot is not significant. What is significant is that she and Richard do not share the same bed. Although "a virginity" is mentioned regarding Clarissa, her relationship with Richard cannot have been entirely celibate, because they have a daughter. Clarissa's feelings about love lead to a new revelation: the statement that Clarissa feels differently about women than about men. This immediately calls up the image of Sally Seton. Clarissa wonders if perhaps she was in love with Sally at Bourton.

Clarissa's memories suggest feelings of bisexuality, and she seems aware of these feelings. Yet some of her thoughts conflict with this interpretation. True, Sally had once kissed Clarissa on the lips, and Clarissa has treasured that moment as a great gift. Yet she also says that her love was "disinterested," unlike the love she would have for a man. Ultimately, Woolf leaves the question of sexuality a mystery, emphasizing the idea that much about a person can never be known.

Study Questions

1. What does Clarissa hand to Lucy?

2. Why would Clarissa have liked to have been invited to Millicent Bruton's lunch party?

3. What word describes Clarissa's bed in the attic?

4. About which moment in Baron Marbot's military career is Clarissa reading?

5. What is Clarissa's first impression of Sally Seton?

6. How had Sally arranged flowers in such a different fashion from what Clarissa's Aunt Helen was accustomed?

7. What quotation from Shakespeare's *Othello* did Clarissa remember in connection with Sally?

8. What did Sally ask from Joseph Breitkopf?

9. What does Clarissa finally decide about her feelings regarding not being invited to Lady Bruton's lunch?

10. What does Lucy offer to do that so pleases Clarissa?

Answers

1. Clarissa hands her parasol to Lucy.

2. Clarissa would have wanted to attend Millicent Bruton's lunch party because they are said to be extraordinarily amusing.

3. "Narrow" is the word used to describe Clarissa's bed in the attic.

4. Clarissa reads about Baron Marbot's retreat from Moscow.

5. Clarissa's first impression of Sally Seton is of Sally sitting on the floor, with her arms around her knees, smoking a cigarette.

6. Instead of using the many little vases in Bourton, Sally had cut the heads off the flowers and made them float in a bowl of water. Clarissa thought that the effect was extraordinary, but her Aunt Helen thought that it was a wicked way to treat flowers.

7. In connection to Sally, Clarissa thought of the quotation "I fit were now to die 'twere now to be most happy."

8. Sally asked Joseph Breitkopf (another guest at Bourton that summer) to tell her the names of the stars.

9. Clarissa finally decides that feeling vain or suspicious about not being invited to Lady Bruton's lunch is utterly base.

10. Clarissa is very pleased by Lucy's offer to mend Clarissa's dress. Clarissa refuses, saying that Lucy has enough on her hands already.

Suggested Essay Topics

1. Do Clarissa's memories of Bourton, in this reading, have in common a mood or subject? Go through this reading section and describe the tone of the memories, drawing comparisons and contrasts along the way. Be sure to include specific points.

2. Clarissa has different reactions to Lady Bruton and her lunch. What does Clarissa's reactions to Lady Bruton tell us about Clarissa? What do you think of these reactions? Why?

Part Four

New Characters:

Peter Walsh: *an old friend of Clarissa's, recently returned from India; He was a suitor of Clarissa's, back in the Bourton days; 53-years-old*

Elizabeth: *Clarissa and Richard Dalloway's 17-year-old daughter*

Summary

Clarissa is mending her dress when she hears voices downstairs. It is Peter, returned from India and dropping in unexpectedly. They are pleased to see each other, yet while the conversation begins comfortably, their eyes, voices, and gestures convey the strong emotions that the reunion sparks.

Peter asks about Richard, and Clarissa mentions her party. Clarissa notices that Peter has kept his old habit of playing with his pocketknife. Part of her feels uneasy with Peter's manner of conversation, for she gets the impression that he is bored.

The conversation turns to Bourton, and they become aware of the past impinging on the present moment. The memories they raise are like ghosts. Clarissa inadvertently alludes to Peter having once proposed to her. She deeply regrets referring to that unhappy moment, which Peter automatically remembers as well. He seems to relive the torment that it caused him. When Clarissa mentions the lake at Bourton, the images it calls up threaten to overwhelm

her. Clarissa asks Peter about his life. He tells her he is in love. Peter watches the effects of his news on Clarissa, and she sees him observing her. True, the woman Peter loves, Daisy, is married, but even so, both Clarissa and Peter feel that this news represents a kind of victory for him.

Both Peter and Clarissa are increasingly aware of how they must appear to the other, and this robs them of their personal balance. Each thinks of him or herself as a failure compared to the other. Peter abruptly bursts into tears. Clarissa comforts him, reflecting that in not choosing him, she has foregone such displays of emotion.

When Peter regains his composure, Clarissa marvels at the change, and sees that he still has a strange kind of power. Curiously enough, Peter, in that same moment, recognizes that Clarissa has a power over him. He seizes her by her shoulders, to forcefully ask her if she has been happy with Richard.

Elizabeth enters at this moment, and Clarissa seizes the interruption to avoid the conversation Peter was starting. Peter, exhausted, greets Elizabeth vaguely and leaves, brushing past mother and daughter. As he leaves, Peter hears Clarissa's reminder about the party echoing in his ears.

Analysis

One of Woolf's themes in this novel is the power of the past in the human mind. Clarissa and Peter might not love each other, yet each feels that the other has power over them. Neither of them seems able to release the past, and each, having made his or her decisions, has doubts and regrets.

The world of Bourton and that particular summer (referred to as "that awful summer" by several of the characters) is resurrected for the reader, and relived by both Clarissa and Peter in this section. Their strongest emotions come not from their present lives, but from the past.

Peter's display of his pocketknife is clearly a phallic image. This is an example of the influence of Freud's theories on Woolf's writing. Freud first described the behavior of displacement, in which personal anxiety manifests itself symbolically. The action of Peter taking out his knife the moment he begins talking with a woman for whom he has strong sexual feelings, emphasizes his unarticulated desires.

Study Questions

1. Who tries to prevent Peter from going upstairs to see Clarissa?

2. What does Clarissa try to hide as she hears footsteps upon the stairs?

3. With whom does Peter say he often wished he had gotten along better?

4. To whom is Peter's beloved already married?

5. Who are the solicitors (lawyers) with whom Peter is arranging Daisy's divorce?

6. From what college was Peter "sent down" (expelled)?

7. To what sudden and odd conclusion does Clarissa come regarding Richard lunching at Lady Bruton's?

8. What words are used to describe the way that Clarissa introduces Elizabeth to Peter?

9. To what is the sound of Big Ben striking the half hour compared?

10. What does Peter stuff into his pocket immediately before leaving?

Answers

1. Lucy tries to prevent Peter from going upstairs to see Clarissa.

2. As she hears footsteps upon the stairs, Clarissa tries to hide the dress she is mending.

3. Peter says he often wished he had gotten along better with Clarissa's father, Justin Parry.

4. Peter's beloved, Daisy, is already married to a Major in the Indian Army.

5. The lawyers with whom Peter is arranging Daisy's divorce are Messrs. Hooper and Grateley.

6. The college from which Peter was expelled is Oxford.

7. The sudden and odd conclusion to which Clarissa comes regarding Richard lunching at Lady Bruton's is that he has left her.

8. The words used to describe the way that Clarissa introduces Elizabeth to Peter are "emotionally" and "histrionically."

9. The sound of Big Ben striking the half hour is compared to "a young man, strong, inconsiderate, indifferent," "swinging dumbbells this way and that."

10. Peter stuffs his handkerchief into his pocket immediately before leaving.

Suggested Essay Topics

1. What factors contribute to the emotions felt by Clarissa and Peter? Which one do you feel has more regrets, and which one is in the better position? Why?

2. How do memories affect Clarissa in this chapter, compared to how they have affected her in the previous chapters? How does memory affect Peter?

Part Five

Summary

Peter leaves, and walks the streets. His mind is reeling from the interviews he has just had with Clarissa. He is upset at her and at himself and wonders about what she and the people in the Dalloways' social circles whom Peter once knew must think of him. Peter asserts that he doesn't care what she and they think of him, yet he still evaluates his life and feels like a failure. As consolation, he reminds himself, he is in love, and in that he is fortunate.

Next there is a meditation from the narrator on the city and time. A clock that follows the tolling of Big Ben is likened to a hostess arriving to her guests.

Peter sees a group of boys in uniform, marching in formation. Peter admires them, yet his feelings are conflicted. He next sees a

young woman, and follows her for a while. He imagines what she might be like, and considers approaching her. When she unlocks a door and disappears behind it, he gives up what he calls "his fun."

Wondering where to go next, Peter finds Regent's Park, where he decides to sit and smoke. Out of nowhere, it seems, he thinks of Elizabeth and decides to speak to her at the party that night. He tosses the cigar, and a sudden need for sleep overcomes him. An old gray nurse with a perambulator (baby carriage) watches him sleep. The narrator gives a meditation on the images of sleep and journeying.

Analysis

This is the reader's first access to Peter's mind, and in it is found the same kind of disorder seen in Clarissa. He is unhappy for reasons very similar to Clarissa's sadness. His thoughts about the past interfere with his present happiness, and his introspection makes him worry about how others perceive him.

This reading section is one of the more abstract in the novel. The narrator's tangents seem not to coincide with the story, yet the pictures of the city and of time and sleep all contribute to the great portrait of the human mind that Woolf strives to convey. There is a great sadness and beauty here, which may be appreciated by reading aloud the text and through analyzing the paragraphs one by one.

Study Questions

1. As Peter walks the street after leaving Clarissa's, what time is it?

2. What question does Peter ask himself regarding Clarissa?

3. At what statue does Peter stare and glare as he thinks of Clarissa and "her set"?

4. What are the boys in uniform carrying?

5. In what famous London square does Peter see the attractive young woman?

6. What does Peter imagine asking the young woman?

7. What does Peter imagine himself to be as he follows the young woman?

8. What does Peter remember about Regent's Park?

9. To what does the narrator liken the old gray nurse?

10. What is the central image of the meditation that follows Peter's having fallen asleep?

Answers

1. As Peter walks the street after leaving Clarissa's, the time is half past eleven.

2. Peter asks himself why Clarissa gives her parties.

3. Peter stands staring and glaring at the statue of the Duke of Cambridge as he thinks about Clarissa and "her set."

4. The boys in uniform are carrying guns.

5. Peter sees the attractive young woman in Trafalgar Square.

6. Peter imagines inviting the young woman to have an ice with him.

7. Peter imagines himself to be an adventurer as he follows the young woman.

8. Peter remembers walking in Regent's Park when he was a boy.

9. To the narrator, the old gray nurse seems like the champion of the rights of sleepers or a spectral presence found in the woods.

10. The central image of the meditation that follows Peter's noonday snooze is that of the solitary traveller.

Suggested Essay Topics

1. Given what we have seen of their thoughts thus far, how do Clarissa's and Peter's memories of Bourton compare? What does each remember, and how do they feel about their memories?

2. What information and viewpoints does the narrator add to the main story of Clarissa and Peter? How do the digressions on time, London, and the solitary traveller relate to the characters?

Part Six

Summary

Peter wakes with the words "the death of the soul." Images crowd thick and fast, as the narrator relates Peter's dreams. The words Peter spoke as he awakened are connected to his dreams about Bourton, and the summer long ago when he loved Clarissa. A minor scandal about class and marriage caused a rift that stuck in Peter's mind. He thinks of it as the beginning of the end for so many perfect friendships. He remembers Clarissa's close relationship with Sally Seton, despite the difficulties that arose between them.

Richard Dalloway comes into Peter's thoughts, as the man he was sure that Clarissa would marry; Peter was right. The pain he felt, even at that moment, was intense, and what happened over the next few days did nothing to lessen it. Even the few happy moments he had were spoiled by his realization that he would lose Clarissa to Richard.

Finally he confronted Clarissa in the garden. Although the conversation is not included by the narrator, its content is implied. His predictions were correct, and Clarissa had shut him out of her emotions.

Analysis

This is the first reading section to take place almost entirely in the past. The narrator explains the past events to which Clarissa and Peter have been referring, from the point of view of Peter's dreams. The explanation does much to explain Peter's feelings during his earlier conversation with Clarissa. The dream summary is like a history lesson. By following what happened long before, we can see why the characters feel as they do now.

Study Questions

1. How does Peter Walsh awaken at Regent's Park?
2. How was the married housemaid who visited Bourton dressed?
3. Whose soul had Peter instinctively decided had died, and why?
4. What was the name of Clarissa's dog?
5. What was the great bond between Peter and Sally?
6. How had Clarissa first introduced Richard Dalloway?
7. What did Sally Seton call Richard Dalloway?
8. What had Peter called Clarissa that caused her discomfort?
9. At what time had Peter asked Clarissa to meet him at the fountain?
10. What had Peter scribbled at the end of the note to Clarissa?

Answers

1. Peter Walsh awakens very suddenly at Regent's Park.
2. The married housemaid who visited Bourton was dressed "like a cockatoo."
3. Peter had decided, instinctively, that Clarissa's soul had died, because of her prudish reaction to the minor scandal of the man and his housemaid.
4. The name of Clarissa's dog was Rob.
5. The great bond between Peter and Sally was that Clarissa's father, Justin Parry, disliked both of them intensely.
6. Clarissa first introduced Richard Dalloway as "Wickham."
7. Sally Seton called Richard Dalloway "My name is Dalloway!"
8. Peter had called Clarissa "the perfect hostess," where upon she winced.
9. Peter had asked Clarissa to meet him at the fountain at three o'clock.

10. Peter had scribbled "Something very important has happened" at the end of the note to Clarissa.

Suggested Essay Topics

1. Summarize Peter's memories. What has he tended to remember, both in terms of specific events and the mood that those events left in his mind?

2. These memories are filled with emotions, mostly Peter's. What are your reactions to his experiences? How did he behave, how could he have handled himself differently, and what do you think he should have done?

Part Seven

Summary

Waking suddenly, Peter considers the park. He sees the Smith couple in their distress.

The story shifts from Peter's point of view to Lucrezia's thoughts. It is almost time for Septimus' appointment with Sir William Bradshaw, the second doctor examining Septimus. Dr. Holmes cannot do anything for Septimus, and calls in the eminent Sir William.

Lucrezia frets over her marriage and her life. Although she wants to love her husband, she is indignant about her suffering, and thinks about the way her life was before Septimus. Lucrezia asks herself why she should suffer so. She knows that Septimus saw horrible things in the war, and lost a close friend, Evans, whom he had met there. However, everyone saw horrible things in the war, and she does not understand her husband's reactions. Her expressions of sorrow alienate Septimus even further. He feels completely alone and trapped.

Septimus experiences many hallucinations, and his state of mind is fragmented, paranoid and delusional. He writes down messages he is convinced are being sent to him, and he feels that his task is to deliver these truths to the world. He is apprehensive about seeing and talking with Evans.

Finally, Lucrezia returns him to reality by reminding him that

they have to be moving on to their appointment. Septimus obeys reluctantly, and wonders if Lucrezia is plotting against him.

Analysis

This reading section provides another window into a character's mind. As we have seen Clarissa's and Peter's mental workings, now we have insights into what makes Septimus tick. The only conclusion we can come to is that his inner clock has malfunctioned.

As mentioned earlier, the psychology of war veterans was unknown in 1923, the year in which *Mrs. Dalloway* is set. World War I was known for its abominable trench warfare, which kept soldiers in such conditions that physically unharmed men went home utterly destroyed by the war. Leonard Woolf and others have said that these sections recreate the psychotic mind, reflecting Virginia Woolf's own fits of madness. Some have suggested that Septimus' fixation on Evans is based on his having fallen in love with Evans, but there is no reliable evidence of this.

Lucrezia is compared to a bird in this reading section, just as Clarissa was thought of as bird-like by Scrope Purvis at the beginning of the novel. The image occurs elsewhere as well, and there are several possible interpretations of this. Birds are generally thought to be free of earthly forces while still at the mercy of the winds. This idea touches on elements of both women.

Study Questions

1. What does Peter Walsh decide regarding Regent's Park?

2. What was little Elise doing before she ran into the woman's legs?

3. What does Lucrezia Smith do when a small child runs into her legs?

4. What doctor had said that there was nothing wrong with Septimus?

5. What does Lucrezia say has grown so thin?

6. What does Septimus imagine is happening to the dog that sniffs at his trousers?

7. What does Septimus imagine is played among the traffic?

8. What word does Septimus think of as splitting its husk?

9. Where are the dead located in the song that Septimus hears Evans sing?

10. What is the name of the dead man at whom Septimus thinks he is smiling?

Answers

1. Peter Walsh decides that Regent's Park hasn't changed very much since he was a boy.

2. Little Elise was finding some pebbles to add to her collection when she ran into the woman's (Lucrezia's) legs.

3. When a small child runs into her legs, Lucrezia Smith picks her up, dusts her little frock, and kisses her.

4. Dr. Holmes had said that there was nothing wrong with Septimus.

5. Lucrezia says that her hand has grown very thin.

6. Septimus imagines that the dog that sniffs at his trousers is turning into a man.

7. Septimus imagines that a boy's elegy is played among the traffic.

8. The word that Septimus thinks of as splitting its husk is "time."

9. In the song that Septimus hears Evans singing, the dead are in Thessaly (a province of Ancient Greece), among the orchids.

10. The name of the dead man at whom Septimus thinks he is smiling is Evans.

Suggested Essay Topics

1. How does Septimus' unhappiness compare with those of Clarissa and Peter? Are there any ways in which Septimus is at an advantage over these other characters? Why or why not?

2.   What are your responses to Septimus' thoughts and feelings? What choices does he have, and what is the best course of action for him to take? Remember to support your reasoning.

Part Eight

New Character:

Sylvia: *Clarissa's late sister*

Summary

Observing Septimus and Lucrezia in their "squabble," Peter feels that he sees a picture of youth. The narrator discloses Peter's history regarding relationships, and his perceptions of his choices. That he had always been too susceptible to impressions is blamed for his troubles, and his moodiness has stayed with him, from adolescence to the present.

Peter sums up the last five years, and the women he has thought about. These thoughts lead to Sally Seton, and how Sally was the most authentic of all the people in Clarissa's circle. Peter appreciated Sally's integrity, and he is surprised that she married a rich man and settled into a conventional life.

The tale of Bourton continues, told in a combination of Peter's and the narrator's points of view. We find that Sally hated Hugh, and Peter agrees with her. (Clarissa had commented in the first reading section that Peter despised Hugh.) Sally and Peter also discussed Richard Dalloway. They met in the garden one night and talked about saving Clarissa from those who would stifle her soul. Still, Peter recognized Richard, even then, as a basically worthy man.

There are many separate incidents and myriad details from those times. Peter denies that he still loves Clarissa. His thoughts run between himself and her, the lives each has built, and how his choices have put him at the mercy of others instead of in control of himself. Peter broods on Clarissa's sister, who was killed accidently by a falling tree. He sums up his feelings about Clarissa, and his outburst at her home.

Analysis

In the middle of his mental journeys through the past is this: "(it was extraordinary how vividly it all came back to him, things he hadn't thought of for years,)". This is an important point. Even if Peter has not thought of these subjects for years, that did not make them go away. In India he may have been too busy to think about Clarissa and memories of Bourton. However, the hurtful memories have been repressed, and his return to London and to people of his past thawed the feelings he had kept frozen.

This would explain his emotional outburst in front of Clarissa. When he thinks about whether he loves Clarissa, he has his pocketknife in his hand. As well as a possible phallic image, this is also a display of hidden or displaced violence, no matter how innocent it may seem.

Clarissa never mentions or thinks about her sister, and this is curious. Although it is possible that Clarissa did not love and does not miss Sylvia, it is likelier that the incident was so traumatic that Clarissa does not think about it at all. Considering Clarissa's unnamed "illness" mentioned in section three, and the connections between the mental illness in the novel and in Woolf's life, perhaps her sister's death harmed Clarissa profoundly.

Study Questions

1. According to Peter's experiences, what happened to one's views about women after coming back from India?

2. What are two of the changes that Peter sees in England in the five years he's been away?

3. In which city is Sally living with her rich husband, much to Peter's surprise?

4. About which antediluvian (ancient) topic does Peter remember Sally and Hugh arguing about at Bourton?

5. What does Peter envision Hugh doing in his job at Court?

6. How much does Peter assume that Hugh earns per year?

7. How much does Peter assume that he must earn per year?

8. What specific event at Bourton summarizes Peter's feelings about Richard?

9. What does Peter remember Sally doing in the garden?

10. Whom does Peter blame for the death of Sylvia, Clarissa's sister?

Answers

1. According to Peter's experiences, one fell in love with every woman one met after coming back from India.

2. Two of the changes that Peter sees in England in the five years he's been away are that people now write about water-closets (bathrooms) in respectable public print, and that young women now apply their makeup in public.

3. Much to Peter's surprise, Sally is living in Manchester with her rich husband.

4. Peter remembers Sally and Hugh arguing about women's rights at Bourton.

5. Peter envisions Hugh polishing Imperial shoebuckles in his job at Court.

6. Peter assumes that Hugh earns five to ten thousand pounds per year.

7. Peter assumes that, with Daisy with him, he must earn at least five hundred pounds per year.

8. The specific event that summarizes Peter's feelings about Richard is of the latter tending to Clarissa's dog, whose paw was badly torn in a trap.

9. Peter remembers Sally tearing a rose in the garden, and admiring the beauty of cabbage leaves.

10. Peter blames Clarissa's father, Justin Parry, for the death of Clarissa's sister, Sylvia.

Suggested Essay Topics

1. What new information about Bourton and the past does the reader learn in this reading section? How does it compare with what was known previously?

2. Focus on Sally Seton. How does what Clarissa said about her previously compare with what we learn about her in this reading section? What constitutes her character, and how does she change?

Part Nine

Summary

Peter's attention is caught by the sounds of an old, ragged woman, singing nonsense. She does not seem rational. The narrator describes how, throughout the entire history of the planet, the woman had stood there and sang this song about a lost love.

Lucrezia (who is called "Rezia" from this point onward) also hears the woman, and pities her. Yet the pity she feels is mostly for herself. Her unhappiness is overtaking her, and her last hope is that Sir Bradshaw can cure Septimus. She decides to be cheerful and optimistic.

The narrator describes Septimus' appearance and history. He is a man who could become either successful or merely a survivor. He had a typically troubled boyhood, and he went to London, a large and impersonal city. He loved literature, and went to public lectures on Shakespeare. He fell in love with the lecturess, Miss Isabel Pole. His supervisor, Mr. Brewer, had great things in mind for Septimus, until the latter had volunteered for the war.

Evans was killed, but Septimus was spared injury, and at the end of the war stayed at an inn in Milan. Lucrezia was the innkeeper's younger daughter, and he proposed to her in a moment of great insecurity.

The two of them strolled in London and watched people's fashions. Septimus sensed Rezia's sense of style, but there were no more delights for him now. Rezia attributed his habits to normal English reserve, and thought nothing of it. Septimus was welcomed back to work by Mr. Brewer, and he read Shakespeare again, but nothing was the same. The world was made of filth, and Shakespeare knew it, yet Rezia wanted to have a son just like Septimus. Her desire for children grates on Septimus.

Septimus' thoughts and perceptions wandered further away. He did not communicate this to Rezia or anyone else. His ability to function declining, he surrendered to outside assistance.

Analysis

The narrator's tangent that begins this reading section may seem highly abstract, but the description of the song and the singer, provides another window into madness. An old woman sings that for a million years, when London was an uninhabitable great swamp, her beloved thought of her. There is a great sadness in this idea. Try to imagine the life of a person who needs to convince herself that this is true. Such is the torment Woolf conveys.

The reader also receives insights into Lucrezia's unhappiness, which may provoke different reactions. After all, she focuses on her own suffering without truly examining Septimus' situation. Septimus' love of Shakespeare is illustrated in the many references to his work throughout the novel. Many of Woolf's characters in *Mrs Dalloway* refer to Shakespeare, as he is one of England's national treasures. Interestingly, each of the characters quotes "The Bard" selectively to agree with particular personal views. Shakespeare is held to believe whatever the characters believe. Woolf's characters use literature to comfort themselves, just as people do in real life.

Study Questions

1. From what location does the nonsense song issue?

2. Who gives the old woman a coin?

3. Why had Septimus left home as a mere boy?

4. Off of what road had Septimus lodged once he first got to London?

5. At what firm is Mr. Brewer, Septimus' supervisor, a managing clerk?

6. What would Lucrezia say matters most?

7. What did Septimus, staring through a train window, think might be possible?

8. Off what road did Septimus and Lucrezia take admirable lodgings in London?

9. What did Septimus decide that Shakespeare loathed?

10. To what did Septimus compare the sound of Lucrezia crying?

Answers

1. The nonsense song issues from the Regent's Park Tube (subway) station.

2. Peter Walsh gives the old woman a coin.

3. Septimus left home as a mere boy because of his mother, who lied.

4. Septimus had lodged near Euston Road once he first got to London.

5. Mr. Brewer is a managing clerk at Sibleys and Arrowsmith's.

6. Lucrezia would say, "It is the hat that matters most."

7. Staring through a train window, Septimus thought it might be possible that the world was without meaning.

8. Septimus and Lucrezia took lodgings off the Tottenham Court Road in London.

9. Septimus decided that Shakespeare loathed humanity.

10. Septimus compared the sound of Lucrezia crying to a piston pumping.

Suggested Essay Topics

1. How is your summary of Septimus altered in this reading section? What new information do you have about him, and how does it affect your feelings about him?

2. Given what you have read in this section and what has come
    before it, what could you suggest to alleviate the difficulties
    between Septimus and Lucrezia? On what are their problems
    of communication based, and what do both characters need
    to do in order to improve the situation? Remember to be
    specific, and support your points from the text.

Part Ten

New Characters:

Dr. Holmes: *as revealed in the narrator's tale of Septimus' illness,
he is recommended by Mrs. Filmer, the Smith's cook*

Sir William Bradshaw: *the eminent and almost godlike doctor
called in to aid Septimus*

Summary

The narrative of Septimus' illness continues. Once he "surrendered" to the influence of others, Dr. Holmes begins to visit. He
advises Septimus to take up hobbies. Yet while others think the
doctor a wonderful man, he becomes a dreaded enemy from
Septimus' point of view, a man whose jovial attitude hides fiend-
ish machinations and a cunning nature.

When Rezia seems to agree with Holmes' advice, Septimus feels
betrayed and abandoned. The voices within him clamor for suicide, for he feels weak, and Septimus strains to hear what he imagines Evans is trying to say. Septimus' fits frighten those around him.
Holmes comes back, but he can do nothing for Septimus. This leads
to the present, when, as Big Ben tolls the noon hour, Sir William
Bradshaw's car approaches.

After some background on Bradshaw, we see his first interview
with Septimus, who is neither cooperative nor completely lucid.
Septimus claims to have committed a great crime, which Rezia
denies. Bradshaw holds a private conference with Rezia, and tells
her that Septimus needs to be in an asylum (though he doesn't use
that word), where he can rest properly. Bradshaw promises to con-
firm these plans between five and six o'clock.

Before leaving, the doctor visits Septimus again, who has been brooding on how human nature has "fallen on him," as if it were a hungry beast. Bradshaw, noting Septimus' serious condition, is detached but not unkind. When he leaves, both husband and wife feel abandoned. Rezia feels forsaken because of her hopes that Bradshaw would cure Septimus.

The narrator explores Bradshaw's personal creed: proportion. Through his love of proportion, he has not only maintained his sanity, but led "an exemplary life." Despite the pitfalls of the world and the human mind, he has never stumbled. Lady Bradshaw, on the other hand, lost her sense of proportion once, fifteen years before. She lost interest in the world, and neglected herself. She departed from society, and had to be brought back. Sir William was the man for this job, as he has been for countless similar tasks of reclaiming lost souls.

Analysis

This reading section serves to underline the distinctions perceived between sanity and madness. Perhaps because of her own mental torments, Woolf portrays Septimus very sympathetically. While some readers may view him as simply a lunatic, he is a man in a great deal of pain.

One way to understand both the duality of sanity and madness as well as Septimus' circumstances is to try to see from his perspective. One might assume that since Septimus is insane there is nothing to learn from him, but this is not the case.

The war affected Septimus' concept of reality. He now perceives certain truths, and feels his duty is to share them with the world. He has no wish to return to the life he had before. Once someone has left the world of "normal" human interaction, his paranoia and psychosis may convince him that others will try to regain the control they once had. Bradshaw's job is to help regulate, and from Septimus' point of view enforce, commonly held standards of normal life. This makes him Septimus' enemy.

The narrator seems to comment on this aspect of Bradshaw, noting Proportion's less pleasant sister is Conversion, who loves to convert, to stamp her features on the faces of the weak and helpless, like Septimus. In this way, Woolf implies that Septimus, unhappy and hallucinatory though he may be, is indeed in danger from Holmes, Bradshaw, and their ilk.

Study Questions

1. Where does Dr. Holmes go when he feels the way he thinks Septimus feels?

2. How many children does Dr. Holmes have?

3. What was the great revelation that Septimus had, and where was Rezia at the time?

4. What did Septimus call Dr. Holmes, when the latter came to visit after Septimus' revelation?

5. Where does Holmes suggest the Smiths go if they have no confidence in him?

6. Where does Bradshaw's son go to school?

7. What did Bradshaw realize the moment he saw Septimus?

8. What gives Bradshaw the impression that Septimus is successful in his career?

9. What, just before leaving, does Bradshaw suggest to Septimus?

10. What observation did Septimus make, once Bradshaw left?

Answers

1. When he feels the way that he thinks Septimus feels, Dr. Holmes goes to the Music Hall.

2. Dr. Holmes has four children.

3. Septimus' great revelation was of Evans' voice speaking to him from behind a screen. Rezia was out shopping at the time.

4. When Dr. Holmes came to visit after Septimus' revelation, the latter called him a brute.

5. Holmes suggests that if the Smiths have no confidence in him (and are rich), they should go to Harley Street (a London street renown for its doctors).

6. Bradshaw's son goes to school at Eton.

7. The moment he saw Septimus, Bradshaw realized that this case was one of extreme gravity.

8. A very generously worded letter from Mr. Brewer, Septimus' supervisor, gives Bradshaw the impression that Septimus is successful in his career.

9. Just before he leaves, Bradshaw suggests to Septimus that he "think as little about himself as possible."

10. As Bradshaw left, Septimus observed that the upkeep of Bradshaw's motor car must cost him quite a lot.

Suggested Essay Topics

1. How are the two doctors, Holmes and Bradshaw, different from each other? Do either or both of them fail the Smiths? How so?

2. What is your impression of Septimus? What new information do you have about him now?

Part Eleven

Summary

The section begins with a meditation on time, and the clock under which Hugh Whitbread, on his way to Lady Bruton's, stops to watch the world around him. He is satisfied with what he sees. He feels confident, aware of his strengths, and does not allow the malice of others to affect his peace.

Lady Bruton considers her lunch guests. She considers Richard clearly superior to Hugh, but she is glad to see them both, to ask their help with a small task. The three sit for a sumptuous lunch before business. Bruton often wonders about what she could have accomplished if only she had been born a man.

During the conversation, Lady Bruton asks about Clarissa, and Richard stops to think about her question. Peter Walsh's return to London is commented upon, and the three take a moment to wonder about him, and how his life seems slightly inferior. Yet Hugh

asks for Peter's address in London, and plans to ask him over for lunch.

Having finished their lunch, the three write the letter that Lady Bruton wishes to have printed in *The Times of London*. Though a capable woman in many respects, Bruton knows that these two men have a superior talent in letter writing. Her idea is to relocate young English couples to Canada. This completed, the men prepare to leave. Richard invites her to the party that night. The moment they leave, Bruton lies down for a nap. Today is Wednesday, she thinks.

Stopping at a streetcorner, Hugh suggests going to the jeweler's. Richard, feeling sluggish after a full lunch on a hot day, agrees. He soon regrets this decision, for he finds Hugh's posturing distasteful. He is listless, but then he seizes on an idea that gives him energy. Richard decides to go home to Clarissa.

Analysis

This section provides insights into both Richard's and Hugh's minds, which are not as complex as those of Clarissa's and Peter's. Richard and Hugh are busy, career-oriented men, without much time for brooding on the past or imagining the worlds of others. This probably helps them to be happier, and even healthier, although not as sensitive to the world around them. Even so, Richard's response to Hugh's behavior at the jeweler's, and his thoughts about seeing Clarissa, show his inner life and his complexity. We see a balance between the types of his thoughts.

Although the discussion of the letter's contents is not included, Lady Bruton's idea is clearly implied, and it raises many questions. Her idea to settle respectable English couples in Canada seems odd. Having lost thousands of men during the war, one might think that England needed all its youth. But if (as was the case) many of the lost men had come from the upper classes, then emigration might have been considered a way of keeping a certain balance in England.

Study Questions

1. Is Hugh described as one who "goes deeply"?

2. Is Miss Brush's brother doing well in South Africa?

3. How does Lady Bruton express her preference for Richard Dalloway over Hugh Whitbread?

4. How old is Lady Bruton?

5. What is Richard Dalloway's opinion of Bruton's idea in the letter?

6. What has Richard Dalloway always meant to do when he has "a moment of leisure"?

7. On the corner of what street do Richard and Hugh pause?

8. What pieces of information is Richard surprised to find that the head jeweler possesses?

9. What does Hugh do that disgusts Richard?

10. What would Richard have said to his son, if he had one?

Answers

1. No, Hugh Whitbread is not described as one who "goes deeply." Hugh is one who only brushes the surfaces of ideas and things.

2. No, Miss Brush's brother is not doing well in South Africa; he is doing poorly in Portsmouth.

3. Lady Bruton prefers Richard Dalloway to Hugh Whitbread because, as she puts it, he is "made of much finer material."

4. Lady Bruton is 62-years-old.

5. Richard Dalloway's opinion of Bruton's idea in the letter is that it is "all stuffing and bunkum," but that there was no harm in it.

6. Richard Dalloway has always meant to write a history of Lady Bruton's family, "whenever he had a moment of leisure."

7. Richard and Hugh pause on the corner of Conduit Street.

8. Richard is surprised to hear that the head jeweler has the measurements of Lady Whitbread's neck, and knows about her tastes in Spanish jewelry.

9. Richard is disgusted by Hugh's manners in the jeweler's, and by his statement that he would buy nothing until the head jeweler had returned.

10. If Richard had a son, he would have told him to find a job.

Suggested Essay Topics

1. Describe the lunch and the lunchers. What do they talk about, and what do these topics of conversation, as well as other details, tell us about the participants?

2. Summarize Richard Dalloway based on what we learn about him in this chapter. How does he speak and think? What are his attitudes, and what do you think of him?

Part Twelve

Summary

Richard decides to bring Clarissa flowers. Crossing London, he thinks intently about her. His thoughts center on her, and her importance to him. He yearns to come to her in just the right way, speaking words of love and showing that he appreciates her.

Big Ben tolls thrice in Clarissa's drawing room. She receives a note asking if she might invite Ellie Henderson to her party, and this nettles her. Clarissa had deliberately not invited Ellie, and dislikes feeling pressured to include her. Thoughts about Doris Kilman, who is praying with Elizabeth in another room, also make themselves felt.

Richard surprises her with flowers, but he cannot bring himself to say what he has been thinking. He wavers on the edge of saying what is in his heart. Yet Clarissa understands, for the flowers and the unexpected visit are themselves enough. Richard mentions that Peter is back, and Clarissa tells him that Peter visited that morning. Richard describes Hugh at lunch and afterwards, while Clarissa still talks about Peter. Their words are at cross purposes, and neither side fully hears the other.

The Dalloways discuss the situation with Elizabeth and Kilman; neither of them is pleased. Richard leaves the room to take a nap.

Clarissa remembers that he is following advice that a doctor gave a long time ago. She ponders what it is in the world that occupies her thoughts, that pleases and sustains her. Though she has few hobbies, it is life itself that pleases and engages her most.

Analysis

This section provides still more insight into Richard's personality. We see that once he focuses on Clarissa, on his way home to her, he becomes very sensitive and sympathetic. His ability to see the details of the world around him is a clear sign of both his intelligence and integrity.

Also, this is the reader's first look at the Dalloways' marriage. Instead of interpretations of one character, here they interact. In their speech and gestures, they are quite different. Richard's practical and businesslike manner contrasts with Clarissa's flighty disposition.

The conversation between husband and wife is very revealing. Notice how, soon after their joy at being together, the communication breaks down. It is difficult to be sure how this deterioration begins: with Clarissa's comment that she might have married Peter? With the Kilman situation? With Richard's thoughts about the party? Richard seems to stop indulging his wife, and he soon leaves the room to take a nap.

Study Questions

1. Whom had Richard and Clarissa not spoken of in years?

2. What does Richard see in Piccadilly Circus (a famous London landmark, comparable to New York's Times Square) that particularly makes him irate?

3. What is Richard doing about the police?

4. How is Richard carrying the flowers for Clarissa?

5. What building does Richard think cannot be denied a certain dignity?

6. What is Richard's response when asked about Ellie Henderson?

7. Where does Clarissa place the flowers Richard brought?

8. What does Clarissa imagine that people do, or will, say about her?

9. About what does Clarissa feel after Peter and Richard had criticized her very unjustly?

10. Of what basic pieces of geographic information is Clarissa ignorant?

Answers

1. Richard and Clarissa had not spoken of Peter Walsh in years.

2. In Piccadilly Circus, Richard sees several small children crossing the street alone.

3. Richard is compiling evidence of police wrongdoings and malpractices.

4. Richard bears the flowers for Clarissa as though they are a weapon.

5. Richard thinks that Buckingham Palace cannot be denied a certain dignity.

6. When asked about Ellie Henderson, Richard is sympathetic, and he implies that she should be invited.

7. Clarissa places the flowers Richard brought in vases on the mantelpiece.

8. Clarissa imagines that people say, or will say, that she is spoiled.

9. Clarissa feels that both Peter and Richard had criticized her very unjustly about her parties.

10. In addition to confusing Armenians, Albanians, and Turks, Clarissa does not know what the Equator is.

Suggested Essay Topics

1. Summarize the Dalloways' marriage. What are its strengths and weaknesses? Would you enjoy such a relationship? Why or why not?

2. At the end of this section, and elsewhere in the novel, Clarissa thinks about how others perceive her. Discuss this tendency. Is it an advantage to her, or a disadvantage, or both? Why or why not?

Part Thirteen

New Character:

Doris Kilman: *a bitter and unhappy woman who spends time with (and might be in love with) Elizabeth Dalloway*

Summary

Elizabeth comes in quietly, reluctant to disturb Clarissa, who is napping. The narrator comments upon Elizabeth's unusual, indeed exotic looks. Miss Kilman waits outside the door, and Clarissa engages in a brief and frigidly polite conversation with her. They are going shopping.

The narrator provides Kilman's story to explain her poverty and her bitterness. Always clumsy and unlucky, she lost her job during the war due to her feelings about Germany. Now an itinerant teacher and, it seems, young lady's companion, she is reduced to charity, and is understandably resentful.

Kilman does not try to hide her attitudes, which are completely obvious to Clarissa. That Clarissa dislikes Kilman's association with her daughter has been apparent throughout the day, and the reader learns just what Clarissa thinks of the woman. The half-hour tolls. Clarissa's thoughts fly from one subject to another.

The novel switches to Kilman's perspective. Her thoughts revolve around two subjects: the people she hates and Elizabeth, about whom she feels very strongly. Kilman recalls her own history, and her present situation. She broods on the duality of flesh and spirit, aware of her unloveliness. They enter the department store, to shop for new petticoats for Miss Kilman. The selection features fancy, frilly wares, and Kilman's choices make the clerk wonder.

The novel moves to Elizabeth's perspective. She finds Kilman pathetic, and yet somehow sympathetic. She thinks Kilman spiritual

and serious-minded, and is distressed by the antagonism between Kilman and Clarissa. The two sit for tea and eclairs. Kilman's emotions regarding Elizabeth threaten her composure. She senses that Elizabeth needs to leave, and Kilman becomes desperate at the idea of losing Elizabeth's company. Finally, Elizabeth leaves.

Analysis

Doris Kilman is a different kind of character than the reader has met previously. She is the first religious figure, and though she comes from a lower social and economic class than the Dalloways, her education and sensibilities are as developed as Septimus', despite her meager income. She may have had a somewhat comfortable childhood, but she is now suffering under economic hardships.

Kilman is similar to Clarissa in at least one important way: neither of them like how they look. Clarissa's physique, however, is deemed more becoming by society's standards. This too provokes Kilman's disdain.

Woolf's long-standing thematic interest in sexuality and obsession are present in her portrayal of Kilman's interest in Elizabeth. Earlier, Clarissa had speculated as to whether Kilman might be in love with Elizabeth, and this seems to be the case.

Study Questions

1. What kind of flower is Elizabeth compared to?

2. With what words does Miss Kilman sum up Richard's and Clarissa's attitudes toward her?

3. What exactly has Miss Kilman been hired to do?

4. Where does Miss Kilman think that Mrs. Dalloway, and all the other fine ladies, should be?

5. What did Clarissa yell to Elizabeth as the latter left?

6. When Clarissa thinks about the destructive power of love, who in particular occurs to her as an example?

7. Why and for how long does Miss Kilman think about Russia?

8. What does Elizabeth feel is the one pleasure left to Miss Kilman?

9. What does Kilman say about parties?

10. What does Kilman say just before Elizabeth leaves?

Answers

1. Elizabeth is compared to a hyacinth.

2. Miss Kilman considers that Mr. Dalloway had been kind, but Mrs. Dalloway had been merely condescending.

3. Mr. Dalloway had hired Miss Kilman to teach Elizabethan history.

4. Miss Kilman thinks that Mrs. Dalloway, and all the other fine ladies, should be working in factories or behind counters.

5. As Elizabeth left, Clarissa yelled to her from the top of the stairs "Remember the party!"

6. When Clarissa thinks about the destructive power of love, Peter Walsh occurs to her as an example.

7. Upset about Clarissa, Kilman thinks about Russia until she reaches a pillar box.

8. Elizabeth feels that the one pleasure left to Miss Kilman is that of food.

9. Kilman says that Elizabeth mustn't let parties absorb her.

10. Kilman says "Don't quite forget me" just before Elizabeth leaves.

Suggested Essay Topics

1. Having heard about Miss Kilman previously, here we see her ourselves, and learn about her attitudes. Compare Miss Kilman's mental picture of Clarissa to the description that some other character has provided of her. Remember to be specific, and to support your points with citations from the novel.

2. Describe Elizabeth, both her appearance and her personality. Are you surprised by anything about her? Does she seem like a typical 17-year-old? Why or why not? Remember to be specific, and to support your points with citations from the novel.

Part Fourteen

Summary

Doris Kilman sits in desolation. Upset, she rocks like a child, and as she leaves, her clumsiness makes her ridiculous. On the street, she sees Westminster Cathedral, which calms and inspires her. Mr. Fletcher, a friend, sees her in the crowd. He views her with pity and compassion, but he fails to stop and talk with her.

Elizabeth waits for a public bus. People have started comparing her to parts of nature, and this bothers her. She has no desire to be noticed, but her unusual, almost oriental looks and her blossoming womanhood, raise the interests of others.

Through the whirl of colors and movement, Elizabeth's thoughts come to the reader. She shows compassion for Kilman, yet she also judges her. Elizabeth mostly revels in the freedom she feels. Unwatched by any guardian, she can go wherever she wishes. The bus sways in its forward motion like a horse. Elizabeth thinks about her future on the way to the Strand, a famous street that links the western section of London to the main city.

Elizabeth knows that the Dalloways do not often go to the Strand, but her curiosity makes the visit an adventure. The world around her is full of activities and mysteries. Seeing all the people's lives before her gives her confidence and stimulates her thoughts about her own future.

The narrator describes the world Elizabeth sees, in its rich flux of diverse emotions and impressions. The world on this summer day, with the sun starting to sink, is magnificent. Yet Elizabeth realizes that she must be home soon, and she looks for a clock. She has delayed her departure, but now she boards an omnibus homeward. A slight veil of cloud encroaches on the sun.

Analysis

This section provides a detailed look at Elizabeth. It also touches on the difference between outer and inner life when looking at people's perceptions of others. The narrator includes details that make her sound like a doll or a statue. This may be how others see her, yet she is mature and inquisitive, and feels somewhat trapped by the adults who regulate her life.

Also, she is not yet accustomed to blindly accept the class differences that make up British society. Her curiosity distinguishes her from all the other characters. Perhaps this is a function of youth.

The section also focuses on aspects of London, as in the beginning of the novel. Typical of Woolf's talent is her ability in the midst of complex patterns of subjective thought to evoke moving descriptions of place and mood.

Study Questions

1. When Elizabeth leaves, whom does Kilman feel has triumphed?

2. Where are the trunks Kilman runs into meant to be taken?

3. Why, according to the narrator, does Mr. Fletcher not stop and talk with Kilman?

4. On what street does Elizabeth wait for an omnibus?

5. According to Clarissa, what does Elizabeth's friendship with Kilman prove?

6. Where is Clarissa as she thinks this?

7. What did Kilman say regarding Elizabeth's future?

8. Why, exactly, does Elizabeth have to be going home?

9. Toward what does Elizabeth walk a little?

10. In what manner does Elizabeth board the Westminster omnibus?

Answers

1. When Elizabeth leaves, Miss Kilman feels that Mrs. Dalloway has triumphed.

2. The trunks Kilman runs into are meant to be taken to India.

3. According to the narrator, Mr. Fletcher does not stop and talk with Kilman because she is unkempt. Besides, he has to be on his way.

4. Elizabeth waits for an omnibus on Victoria Street.

5. According to Clarissa, Elizabeth's friendship with Kilman proves that Elizabeth has a heart.

6. As she thinks this, Clarissa is reading in bed at three in the morning.

7. Regarding Elizabeth's future, Kilman said that every profession is open to women of her generation.

8. Elizabeth must be going home in order to dress for dinner.

9. Elizabeth walks a little toward St. Paul's.

10. Elizabeth boards the Westminster omnibus "calmly and competently."

Suggested Essay Topics

1. Summarize Elizabeth's feelings about Miss Kilman. How does her view differ from her mother's view? Does Elizabeth see both good and bad qualities in Kilman? What are they?

2. What new information and insights does the reader learn about Elizabeth in this section? Are your feelings about her confirmed, or changed? Why or why not?

Part Fifteen

Summary

Watching the interplay of light and shadow, Septimus is not afraid. His smiling disturbs Rezia, who wonders, feeling that it has nothing to do with their marriage.

The narrator describes Septimus' reactions to different events, and how he shows strong emotions suddenly. In a world filled with hidden taunts, all things mean something else, and noble ideas mean nothing.

He comes back, slowly, to the present moment. Rezia is making a hat for Mrs. Peters. He speaks lucidly, and Rezia is grateful. He makes a joke and she is overjoyed. They work on the hat together. Rezia is called away momentarily. For a long moment, Septimus is happy. When it passes, he feels abandoned again. His thoughts are thrown into turmoil, and Evans visits the room.

Rezia returns, but Septimus is lost again. She does not notice; she is busy enjoying the moment that has just past. She feels that life has returned to normal.

Septimus feels that Bradshaw had no right to give orders. He steps into their lives and decrees what "must" be. Rezia brings Septimus his writings. She will keep them safe. Husband and wife share a moment of true connection.

There are voices below, and Dr. Holmes is coming up. Rezia stands in the doorway to block the doctor. She is protecting Septimus as would a mother hen. Meanwhile, Septimus hops around in his anxiety. Loathe to submit to Holmes and the human nature he represents, Septimus considers different methods of suicide. He sees the breadknife and the gas, but these will not do. Ironically, Septimus does not, at that moment, wish to commit suicide. But it seems to be the only escape. To avoid Dr. Holmes, he kills himself by jumping onto the iron palings around the building.

Dr. Holmes sees it, as does Rezia a moment after. Everyone is upset, and they move clumsily in their distress. Big Ben tolls six o'clock. People think to distract themselves, or they retreat into their memories. Mrs. Filmer appreciates the doctor's ability to take charge of the situation. He says Rezia must sleep.

Analysis

This and the previous section draw the day to its conclusion. What we have seen of Septimus has not given us much hope for his health and happiness. He is tragic in the same way that characters in Ancient Greek plays are tragic: he cannot overcome his hardships. Yet, ironically, Septimus is clearly improving before he dies. He re-enters the world on his own, and he feels in control of himself. Also, he does not wish to kill himself, but he feels trapped by the wills of the doctors, which represent the human nature he

detests. We may feel that if he had had more time, he might have found his way to peace. Ambiguity is a major strength of the novel. Woolf does not give the reader easy answers, about Septimus or any of the other characters. Was Clarissa right to reject Peter and marry Richard? Is Septimus entirely crazy, or is it merely that his conception of reality differs from that of others? These are problematic matters of interpretation and discussion.

Study Questions

1. Exactly what, according to Septimus' perceptions, is Nature signifying?

2. What did both Holmes and Bradshaw say was the worst thing for Septimus?

3. What did Mrs. Filmer give Rezia that morning?

4. What does Septimus say about the hat for Mrs. Peters?

5. Why does working on the hat make Septimus proud of it?

6. What was the doom that Septimus had sensed in Milan?

7. Of what had Septimus reminded Rezia when she first saw him?

8. With what does Rezia tie up the bundle of Septimus' drawings?

9. What does Dr. Holmes call Septimus?

10. Whom does Dr. Holmes say is to blame for the suicide?

Answers

1. According to Septimus' perceptions, Nature is signifying an elusive gold spot.

2. Both Holmes and Bradshaw said that excitement was the worst thing for Septimus.

3. Mrs. Filmer gave Rezia grapes that morning.

4. Septimus says that the hat for Mrs. Peters is too small.

5. Working on the hat makes Septimus proud because it is real and substantial.

6. The doom Septimus had felt in Milan was that he would be alone forever.

7. Septimus reminded Rezia of a young hawk when she first saw him.

8. Rezia ties up Septimus' drawings with a piece of silk.

9. Dr. Holmes calls Septimus a coward.

10. Dr. Holmes says that no one is to blame for the suicide.

Suggested Essay Topics

1. Describe Septimus' moods and actions in this section. How does he begin, and what changes does he go through? What happens to change his feelings?

2. Describe Rezia's moods and actions in this section. How does she begin, and what changes does she go through? What happens to change her feelings?

Part Sixteen

Summary

As Peter Walsh walks the streets, he compares England and India. He sees an ambulance, which is going to the Smith's home. He is wondering about himself, about Clarissa, and marriage. She has had a great presence and influence in his life. He enters his hotel, collects his mail, and goes to his room. One of the letters is from Clarissa, saying how nice it was to see him and how he should come to the party. Her efficiency annoys him, for she must have mailed it immediately.

The narrator describes Peter, who thinks about Daisy. Their separation may make her reconsider their relationship. He broods on love, women, Clarissa and Daisy, but most of all on himself. Then he goes down to dinner, and the narrator sets the scene. At dinner Peter wins the respect of those around him. The people at the next table initiate a conversation with him. To them, Peter looks like a successful, worldly man, who understands what goes on around him. Peter looks forward to the party now. He wonders about whom he will talk to, what subjects he should cultivate.

The narrator depicts the evening. Because of the balmy weather, people are dining outdoors, or strolling through the streets. Peter remarks on the changes in London. He walks to Clarissa's party in Westminster. He watches the activity, notes the heat and the humanity, and feels that the world is rich and lovely. He buys a paper, and sees what Septimus saw: that Surrey is "all out"; their cricket team lost. He feels that cricket helps make life bearable. As he approaches Clarissa's, he mentally prepares himself for the party.

Analysis

The section continues the examination of Peter Walsh. We see that others admire him, when we ourselves might not do so. That they think him impressive reveals the gap between how we know ourselves and how others see us. Peter knows himself to be at the mercy of his own thoughts (much as Clarissa does).

When Peter wonders about his future with Daisy, his concerns focus on what others will think of her. This highlights a major theme in the novel: placing value on what other people think. Consider two other women, both mentioned very briefly, who illustrate this issue. In the second section, an Irish woman almost salutes the passing car with a bunch of roses. She resists doing so because a policeman is watching her. In the ninth section, Peter gives a coin to a singing woman, whom people assume is crazy. Her response is, "and if people should see, what matter they?" Clarissa is unhappy when she considers how others see her, while Peter is annoyed by the same thoughts. At seventeen years of age, Elizabeth feels the pressure of this unpleasant reality. As we will see in the next section, the novel has only one character who at any point in her life, acted freely, unmindful of what people thought of her.

A fundamental tension in the novel results from the complexity of human relationships, and with the force of one's own past on present happiness. Although the war has ended, many people fight for their own happiness every day.

Study Questions

1. What does Peter think that one might do in privacy?

2. Who had influenced Peter more than Clarissa had?

3. Did Peter need much effort to read one of Clarissa's letters?

4. What does Peter think he would do when he retires?

5. What does Peter realize has been his undoing?

6. Does Peter decide that he is jealous by temperament?

7. What specific words uttered by Peter win him the respect of others?

8. What does Peter want to ask Richard at the party?

9. What news are the paperboys proclaiming?

10. What does the narrator say the brain and body must do, as Peter approaches the party?

Answers

1. Peter thinks that one might do as one chooses in privacy.

2. No one had influenced Peter more than Clarissa had.

3. Yes, Peter needs "a devil of an effort" to read one of Clarissa's letters.

4. Peter thinks he would write books when he retires.

5. Peter realizes that his being dependent on others has been his undoing.

6. Yes, Peter decides that he is uncontrollably jealous by temperament.

7. The specific words that win Peter the respect of others are "bartlett pears."

8. Peter wants to ask Richard what the conservatives are doing about India.

9. The paperboys are proclaiming a heat wave.

10. The narrator says that the brain must wake, and body contract, as Peter approaches the party.

Suggested Essay Topics

1. We have seen Peter at several points throughout the novel. How have your thoughts about him changed? What do you know about him now that you didn't before?

2. Given what you have seen from the characters, how would you see Peter acting at the party? How would he be received by the different people who have thought about him?

Part Seventeen

Summary

The Dalloways' home is full of commotion. The staff (both the regular servants and those hired for the party) does not want to disappoint their hostess. Mrs. Walker, the cook, feels the most pressure; the Prime Minister is expected.

Mr. Wilkins announces people as they come in. Important figures of London society begin to arrive, yet Clarissa feels sure that the party will be a failure. Seized with worry, she asks herself why she does it. Her answer: better to live and risk than to fade away.

Clarissa sees Peter but does not greet him. His ability to make her judge herself makes her uneasy, especially now. Ellie Henderson, alone and wondering about what she sees, appears pleasant yet hopeless. Richard takes pity on her, and she is grateful. When Peter greets Richard the two start to talk.

An insignificant gesture reassures Clarissa about the party. More people are announced. Sensing that the party has a life of its own, she sees that giving parties makes her step outside herself. She watches people and mingles with them in a new way.

Lady Rosseter is announced, and Clarissa does not recognize the name. It is Sally Seton, and Clarissa is overjoyed. Sally has lost that specialness about her, and is not the same as she was.

But Clarissa is pulled away, for the Prime Minister has arrived. The party is slightly hushed with respect for the honor he bestows upon them all. Clarissa personally introduces him to the guests. The man looks quite ordinary, yet he has a profound effect on the guests.

Peter Walsh watches with contempt. Seeing Hugh confirms his feelings that society life is hypocritical. He sees Lady Bruton thank Hugh for something. The Prime Minister leaves soon, and Clarissa goes back to her guests. She asks Peter to talk with her aunt, Helen Parry. Sally greets Peter, and they begin to talk. Clarissa cannot reminisce with them, for she has hostess duties. The narrator hearkens back to Bourton, the past that hovers in their minds.

Analysis

This section shows the complexity of relationships, through Clarissa's hospitality and the impressions of the myriad guests. We have heard many of the names before, but many are new. The entire spectrum of emotions is revealed by the characters and the narrator. The party is like a picture of the world full of people who love, hate, laugh, and work. It is possible to reconstruct a great deal about human loyalty and hatred through the narrator's comments.

Beyond the present confusion, the section lets the reader benefit from learning about the past. Having read about what Clarissa, Sally, and Peter once shared at Bourton, we know them better. Now, having thought of each other many times, they are reunited. Behind their laughter are strong feelings about the past, and judgments about their own and each other's present lives. Woolf evokes the tension in them all, as well as the happiness.

The curtains are yellow with a bird of paradise pattern. This bird pattern follows the symbolism of comparing women to birds, which runs throughout the novel.

Study Questions

1. What is Lucy's reaction to seeing Elizabeth dressed for the party?

2. What has Mr. Dalloway sent for from the Emperor's cellars?

3. How does Clarissa greet everyone at the party?

4. Is Peter pleased that he came to the party?

5. What is the minor gesture that reassures Clarissa about the party?

6. What is the main thing that makes Ellie Henderson afraid and nervous?

7. How are Ellie and Clarissa related?

8. What do the guests feel as they see the Prime Minister enter?

9. What does Clarissa say that she would like to have had at the party?

10. What does Lady Bruton feel that Richard Dalloway's marriage cost him?

Answers

1. Seeing Elizabeth looking so lovely, Lucy couldn't take her eyes off her.

2. Mr. Dalloway has sent for tokay (a variety of brandy) from the Emperor's cellars.

3. Clarissa greets everyone at the party with "how delightful to see you!"

4. No, Peter is not pleased that he came to the party. He tells himself he should have stayed in and read, or gone to the music hall.

5. The minor gesture that reassures Clarissa about the party is when someone pushes a curtain that billowed with air.

6. The main thing that makes Ellie Henderson afraid is living on three hundred pounds a year.

7. Ellie and Clarissa are cousins. Even so, Ellie understands that Clarissa might not have wanted to invite her to the party.

8. As they see the Prime Minister enter, the guests feel the pride and comfort of seeing a symbol of majesty.

9. Clarissa says she would like to have had dancing at the party.

10. Lady Bruton feels that Richard Dalloway's marriage cost him a chance for the cabinet.

Suggested Essay Topics
1. Describe the mood of the party. What kinds of activities and relationships are being played out there? How does it compare to parties that you yourself have attended?
2. Given what you have read about Sally Seton, are you surprised by what we learn about her in this section? How has she changed? How do Clarissa and Peter respond to her?

Part Eighteen

Summary

Sir and Lady Bradshaw arrive late and apologetic at Clarissa's party. She greets them, though she is not very fond of this couple. She sees in Sir William a man at the peak of his career, wearied by the misery he has seen. Yet she perceives his cold detachment. He talks with Richard about a recent case. Lady Bradshaw tells Clarissa how, as they were leaving, a call came about a suicide. The news shatters Clarissa. Feeling that death has invaded the party, she goes to an empty room. She is upset at the Bradshaws for introducing the subject; the fact that it was a suicide is the worst part.

She understands the choice of suicide. Her busy habits and parties seem like unworthy trifles, while suicide is a statement about life. She senses the great chasm between those who make this statement and herself.

Life with Richard is good, and she is happy. Yet Clarissa admires the man who killed himself, and she feels a kinship with him. The party is ending, and she will go to bed soon, but she must go to Sally and Peter. They compare the past to the present. Peter wanted to write, but never did. Sally had fire in her, but it mellowed. They think about Clarissa and what she became.

People are leaving. Peter shares more with Sally, and they wonder where Clarissa has gone. Their conversation turns to those still at the party, and they comment on Elizabeth. Richard hardly recognizes her. Playing with his pocketknife, Peter waits for Clarissa. Sally leaves, but Peter remains for a moment, aware of the joy and terror in his heart when Clarissa reappears.

Analysis

Though Clarissa was not obsessing about the party during the day, it clearly bothered her. The party is her way of expressing herself, of participating in the world, but at the same time it is a great risk to her self-esteem. The party went well, and in this section dies a slow death, as guests leave and conversations end.

Outside of Septimus, whose story is resolved, the main force of the novel is the legacy of Bourton. This section does not finish those tales, for the characters will go on and have their failures and some triumphs as well. But the past serves to contextualize the present, and it helps us understand the day in the lives of these "people."

Far more than most novels, *Mrs. Dalloway* concentrates on how people are the product of their decisions, and that the greatest threat to happiness is other people. Even more destructive is obsessively valuing other people's perception of us.

Many small details remain mysterious, but overall the novel ends with a feeling of closure. In Peter, the readers see what the characters have perceived: the potential of love to undermine one's mental constitution.

Study Questions

1. Is Bradshaw making a connection between what delayed him and politics?

2. About what had the Prime Minister and Lady Bruton been talking?

3. Into what had Clarissa once thrown a shilling?

4. What surprised Clarissa when she looked out her window?

5. How had Sally once described the cauliflower leaves at Bourton?

6. What is the only thing that Peter knew about Sally's husband?

7. According to Sally, had Hugh once kissed her?

8. Had Sally ever invited the Dalloways to come for a visit?

9. What does Peter say has spoiled his life?

10. What does Sally say about Clarissa and Richard that made Peter protest on Richard's behalf?

Answers

1. Yes, Bradshaw is making a connection between what delayed him and politics. He is talking to Richard about a Bill concerning the victims of shellshock, which influenced the suicide.

2. The Prime Minister and Lady Bruton had been talking about India.

3. Clarissa had once thrown a shilling (a small coin) into the Serpentine River.

4. When she looked out her window, Clarissa was surprised to see the old woman whom she had observed before staring back at her.

5. Sally had once described the cauliflower leaves at Bourton as being "like rough bronze."

6. The only thing that Peter knew about Sally's husband was that he wore two camellias on his wedding day.

7. Yes, according to Sally, Hugh had once kissed her, on the lips, at Bourton. She was outraged.

8. Yes, Sally had invited the Dalloways, year after year, to come for a visit, but they never did.

9. Peter says that his relations with Clarissa spoiled his life.

10. Sally said that Clarissa had cared more for him (Peter) than she ever had for Richard.

Suggested Essay Topics

1. Summarize the conversation between Sally and Peter. How do they talk to each other? Why do they talk the way they do, and what do they accomplish?

2. What do you think about Clarissa's reaction to Septimus'
   suicide? Does it surprise you? What does it tell you about
   Clarissa, and how does it change your reaction to her?

Sample Analytical Paper Topics

The following paper topics are based on the entire book. Following each topic is a thesis and a sample outline. Use these as a starting point for your paper.

Topic # 1

Pick three of the characters and summarize why they might be unhappy. Then compare your findings: What do these factors have in common? How do the characters respond to what bothers them?

Outline

I.   Thesis Statement: *Each of the main characters is unhappy about some aspect of his or her life. These subjects vary widely, yet are comparable.*

II. Clarissa is unhappy about how she appears to others.

    A.   She feels that she is unattractive.

    B.   She feels unpopular.

    C.   She feels that her parties may be a shallow interest.

    D.   She lacks confidence.

III. Peter Walsh is unhappy about the choices he has made.

    A.   He loved Clarissa, but lost her.

     B.   He is in love with a married woman, which is complex.

     C.   He has not followed a straight course of career.

     D.   He feels that he has no foundation in life.

IV.   Lucrezia Warren Smith is unhappy about her marriage.

     A.   She feels that Septimus does not want to get better.

     B.   She wants to have children.

     C.   She thinks about her life before she was married.

     D.   She feels abandoned and cut off from what she knows.

Topic #2

Pick a relationship between two characters and discuss it. How do these two characters know each other, and how has their history together progressed? What mistakes have they made in knowing the other?

Outline

I.   Thesis Statement: *The relationships between two characters show the histories of the individuals involved, and the triumphs and mistakes they have made.*

II.   Clarissa and Peter

     A.   Peter once loved Clarissa, but she married Richard.

     B.   She hardly thinks of Peter, but he thinks of her all the time.

     C.   Having lived in India, he now loves a married woman.

     D.   When they see each other, they feel strong emotions.

III. Clarissa and Richard

     A.   Richard's stability complements Clarissa's flightiness.

     B.   Richard, somewhat unemotional, allows his wife privacy.

     C.   They have different interests.

     D.   They do not seem to communicate much, but when Richard brings flowers, we see a deep bond.

IV. Clarissa and Sally

    A.   Sally is an important part of Clarissa's memories.

    B.   Clarissa thinks she might have been in love with Sally.

    C.   Sally shows up unexpectedly at Clarissa's party.

    D.   Sally has changed, and, although she has often invited Clarissa for a visit, the latter has declined.

Topic #3

The descriptions of London contrast with the interior landscapes of many of the characters. How do the histories of the city and of the characters create their current situations?

Outline

I.   Thesis Statement: *Both London and the characters living within it are the products of their pasts.*

II.   London is peaceful.

    A.   All the descriptions of the city emphasize the serenity.

    B.   Even so, everyone has fresh memories of the recent war.

    C.   When an airplane is heard, people become tense automatically.

    D.   People rely on their traditions of rulers and empire.

III. Clarissa Dalloway's past is in Bourton.

    A.   The home she grew up in is important to her.

    B.   She feels that her daughter is in religious trouble.

    C.   She is not sure that her life has meaning.

    D.   The answers to her problems are within her control.

IV. Peter Walsh's past is an important part of his present.

    A.   Peter thinks about Clarissa often.

    B.   He admits that his feelings about her have had a negative effect on his life.

    C.   Others think that his life has been a failure.

    D.   At the same time, he knows that there is something different, and special, about himself.

Bibliography

Allen, Walter. *The Modern Novel in Britain and the United States.* EP Dutton & Co., New York. 1964.

Johnson, Manly. *Virginia Woolf.* Frederick Ungar Publishing Co., New York. 1978.

Naremore, James. *The World Without A Self: Virginia Woolf and the Novel. Yale* University Press, New Haven CT. 1973.

Woolf, Virginia. *Mrs. Dalloway.* Harcourt Brace & World, New York. 1953.

Woolf, Virginia. *A Writer's Diary.* Edited by Leonard Woolf. Harcourt, Brace and Company. New York. 1954.

Available at your local bookstore or order directly from us by sending in coupon below.

REA's Test Preps
The Best in Test Preparatio

- REA "Test Preps" are far **more** comprehensive than any other test preparation series
- Each book contains up to **eight** full-length practice exams based on the most recent ex
- **Every** type of question likely to be given on the exams is included
- Answers are accompanied by **full** and **detailed** explanations

REA has published over 60 Test Preparation volumes in several series. They include:

Advanced Placement Exams (APs)
Biology
Calculus AB & Calculus BC
Chemistry
Computer Science
English Language & Composition
English Literature & Composition
European History
Government & Politics
Physics
Psychology
Spanish Language
United States History

College Level Examination Program (CLEP)
American History I
Analysis & Interpretation of Literature
College Algebra
Freshman College Composition
General Examinations
Human Growth and Development
Introductory Sociology
Principles of Marketing

SAT II: Subject Tests
American History
Biology
Chemistry
French
German
Literature

SAT II: Subject Tests (continued)
Mathematics Level IC, IIC
Physics
Spanish
Writing

Graduate Record Exams (GREs)
Biology
Chemistry
Computer Science
Economics
Engineering
General
History
Literature in English
Mathematics
Physics
Political Science
Psychology
Sociology

ACT - American College Testing Assessment

ASVAB - Armed Service Vocational Aptitude Battery

CBEST - California Basic Educational Skills Test

CDL - Commercial Driver's License Exam

CLAST - College Level Academic Skills Test

ELM - Entry Level Mathematics

ExCET - Exam for Certificatio Educators in Texas

FE (EIT) - Fundamentals of Engineering Exam

FE Review - Fundamentals of Engineering Review

GED - High School Equivalenc Diploma Exam (US & Cana editions)

GMAT - Graduate Manageme Admission Test

LSAT - Law School Admissio

MAT - Miller Analogies Test

MCAT - Medical College Adm Test

MSAT - Multiple Subjects Assessment for Teachers

NTE - National Teachers Exam

PPST - Pre-Professional Skills

PSAT - Preliminary Scholastic Assessment Test

SAT I - Reasoning Test

SAT I - Quick Study & Review

TASP - Texas Academic Skil Program

TOEFL - Test of English as a Foreign Language